MW01600413

Thank you to the generous te..... ....g....
and talents to make this book possible:

Author
Jane Kurtz

Illustrators
Joanne Stanbridge,
Clark College ECD (Economic and
Community Development), Vancouver:

Lee Baughman
Katie Bradley
Debbie Caton
Cheri Gavin
Suzy Foster

Sue Kramer
Tina Mae Fels
Joyce Saulsbury
Joanne Stanbridge
Irina Sztukowski

Creative directors
Caroline Kurtz, Jane Kurtz,
and Kenny Rasmussen

Translator
Ahmed Dedo Gemeda

Designer
Beth Crow

Ready Set Go Books, an Open Hearts Big Dreams Project

Special thanks to Ethiopia Reads donors and staff for believing in this project and helping get it started-- and for arranging printing, distribution, and training in Ethiopia.

ISBN: 979-8694669412
Library of Congress Control Number: 2020919819

Publication Date: 10/13/20

Lalibela

Laaliibalaa

English and Afaan Oromo

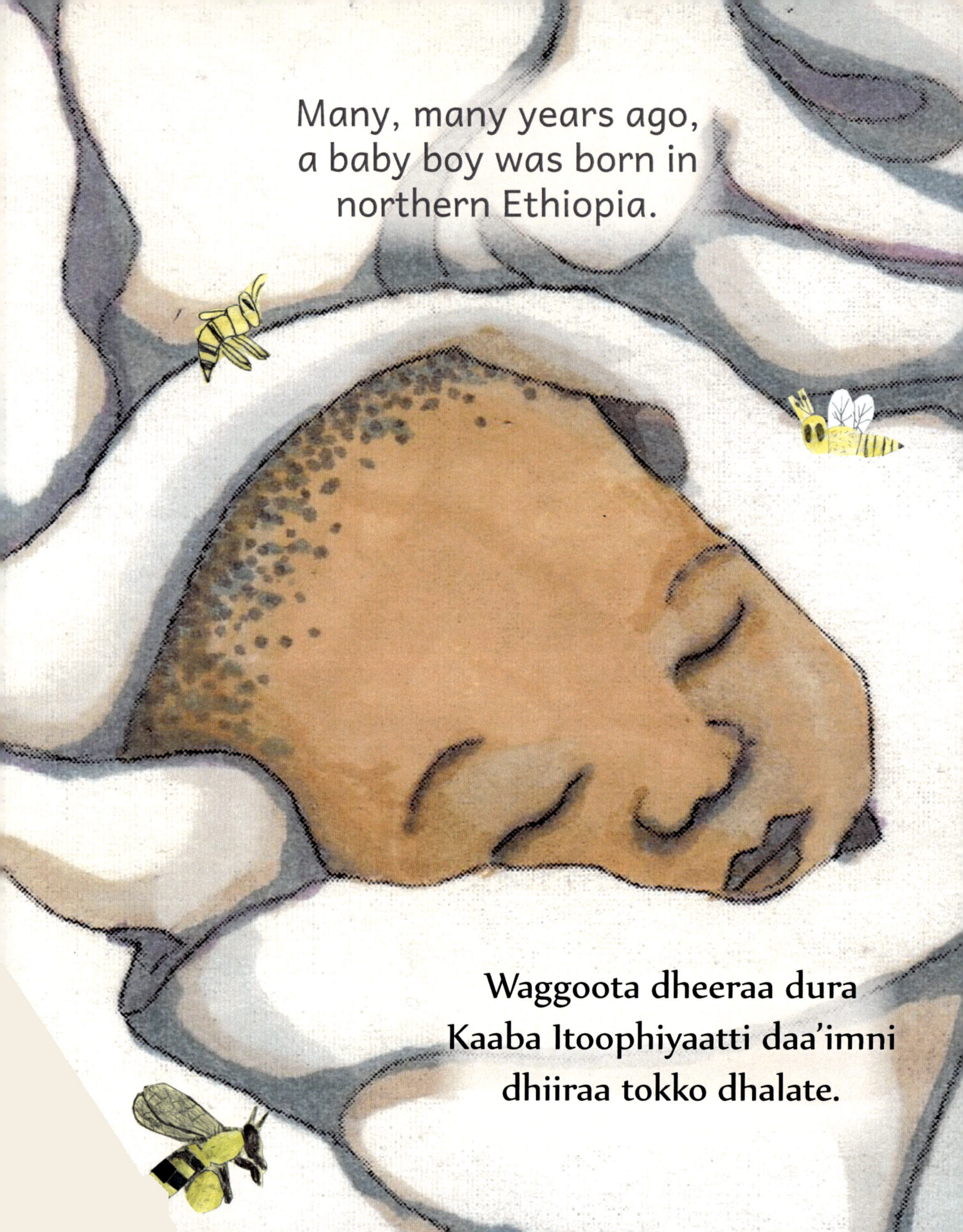

Many, many years ago,
a baby boy was born in
northern Ethiopia.

Waggoota dheeraa dura
Kaaba Itoophiyaatti daa'imni
dhiiraa tokko dhalate.

The stories say that
bees filled the air
around him.

Akka oduu-duriin himutti, qilleensi naannoo
isaa jiru kanniisaan kan guutame ture.

His mother named him Lalibela,
which means the bees honor him.

Harmeen isaa Laaliibalaa jettee maqaa isaa moggaaste.
Hiikni isaas Kanniisonni kan isa jaalatan jechuudha.

Lalibela grew up to be a king with a very big dream of creating a holy city like Jerusalem.

Laaliibalaan, mul'ata magaala qulqulluu akka Iyyeerusaalem bocuu jedhu qabatee guddachuun mootii ta'u danda'e.

The king knew that the shape of
a building can tell a story.

Mootiichi bocni gamoo seenaa
himuu akka danda'u nibeeka ture.

He wanted people to know stories of the Bible even if they could not read.

Namoonni dubbisuu danda'uu baataniis seenaawwan macaafa qulqulluu akka beekanif hawwii qaba ture.

The workers carved huge buildings from solid red rock.

Hojjeettonni dhagaa guddaa diimaa tokko bocanii gamoo guddaa hojjeetan.

They shaped doors, windows, tunnels, and steps, creating eleven churches.

Balbaloota, foddaawwan, holqa keessa daddarbanii fi sadarkaa itti bahan hojjeechuun manneen kiristaanaa kudha-tokko ijaaran.

Today, Ethiopia has many priests.

Har'a Itoophiyaan luboota hedduu qabdi.

Ethiopia also has
many churches.

Itoophiyaan, manneen
kiristaanaa hedduu qabdi.

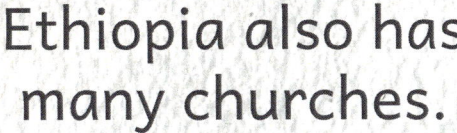

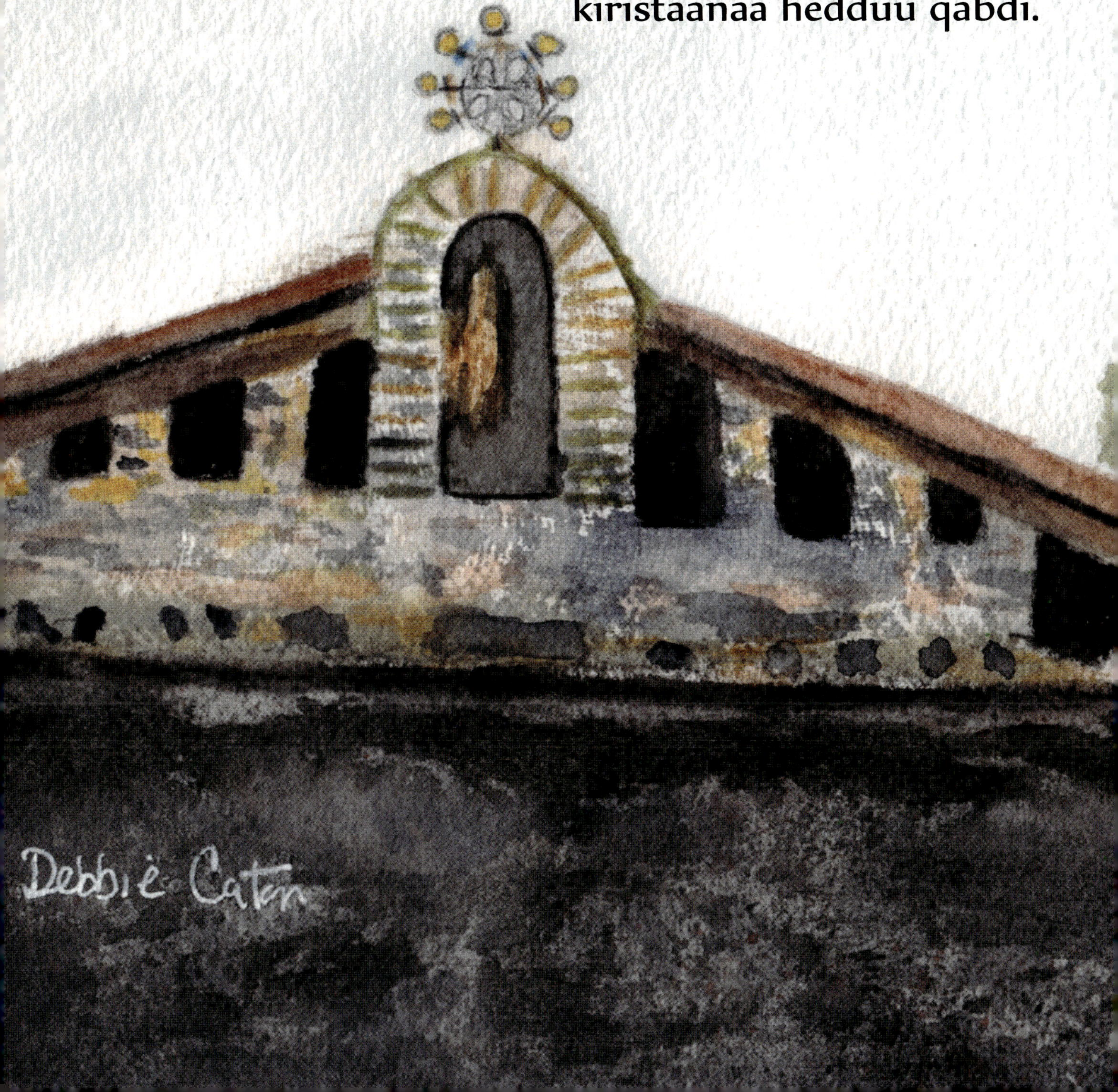

Debbie Caton

But the churches that King Lalibela
dreamed stand out from all the rest.

Haata'u malee, manni kiristaanaa mul'ata
mootii laaliibalaatiin yaadame ijaarame
warreen kaan caalaa ifee mul'ata.

Many pilgrims come from all over Ethiopia
to see the stories carved in stone.

Namoonni bakkeewwan qulqulli amantaa
deeman guutuu Itoophiyaarraa seenaa dhagarraa
bocame kana daawwachuuf nidhufu.

Stories are also told by drums.

Seenaan dibbeedhaan
irra deebi'ee himama.

Stories are told by crosses.

Seenaan fannoowwaniin himama.

Stories are told by priests and deacons.

Seenaan lubootaa fi daaqonootaan irra deebi'ee himama.

Some people spend their lives praying
beside the amazing churches.

Namoonni muraasni manneen kiristaanaa
ajaa'ibsisoo ta'an kanneen akkasii biratti
kadhachuun umrii isaanii fixu.

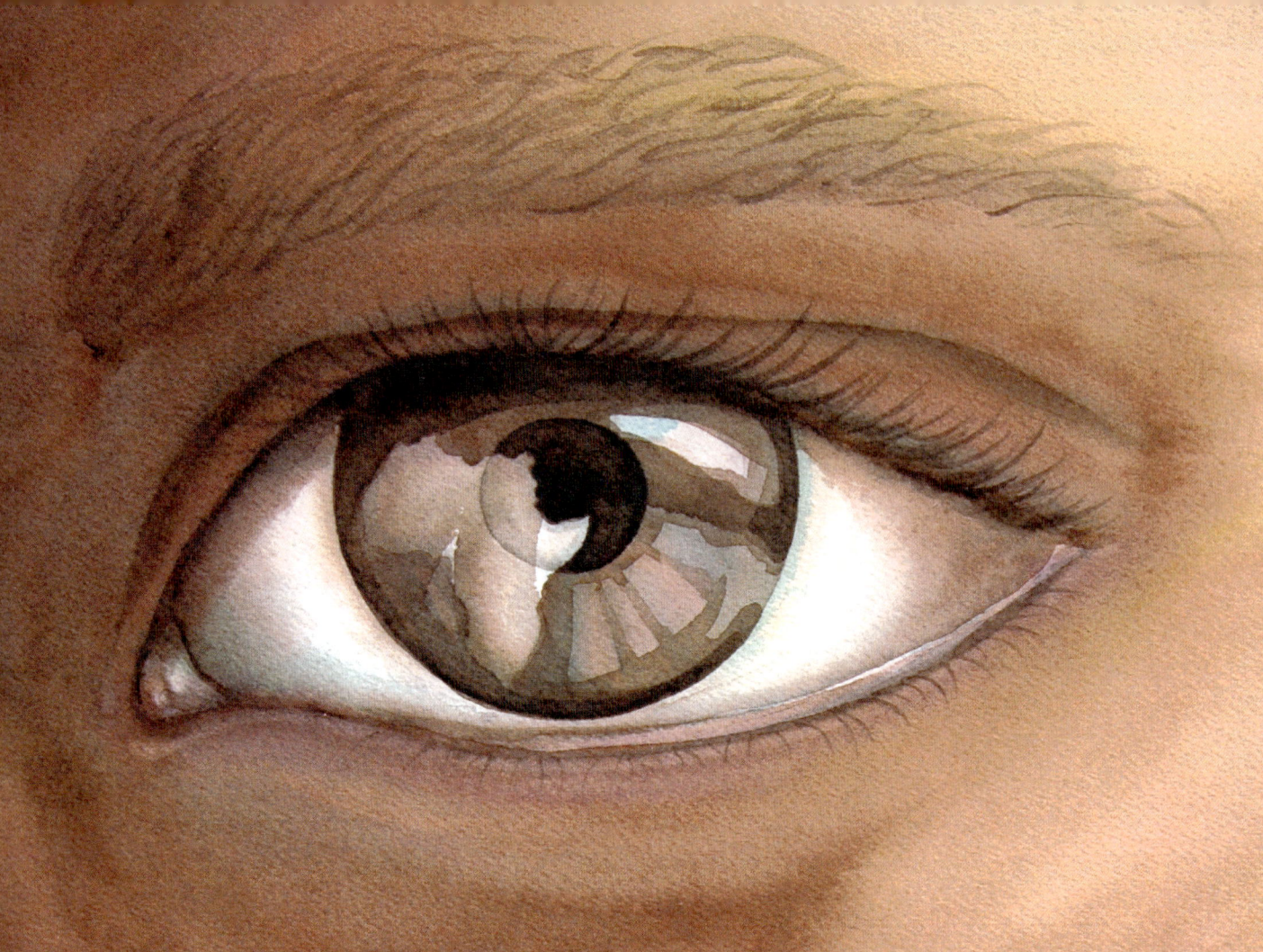

Other people travel from far-away
continents all the way to Ethiopia just
to see the famous Lalibela churches.

Namoonni hedduun kutaalee addunyaa
baay'ee fagoo ta'an garaagaraa irraa imaluun
manneen kiristaanaa Laaliibalaa dinqisiisoo
ta'an kana daawwachuuf gara Afrikaa dhufu.

K. Bradley

They leave gifts in the
churches to say thank you.

Galateeffachuuf kennaawwan garaagaraa
manneen kiristaanichaa keessatti ni kaa'u.

They breathe the holy air of the place where King Lalibela looked at red rock and dreamed a New Jerusalem.

Mootiin Laaliibalaa iddoo dhagaa diimaa ilaaluun Iyeerusaalem ishee haaraa ijaaruf kaayyeeffatetti argamuun qilleensa qulqulluu f.

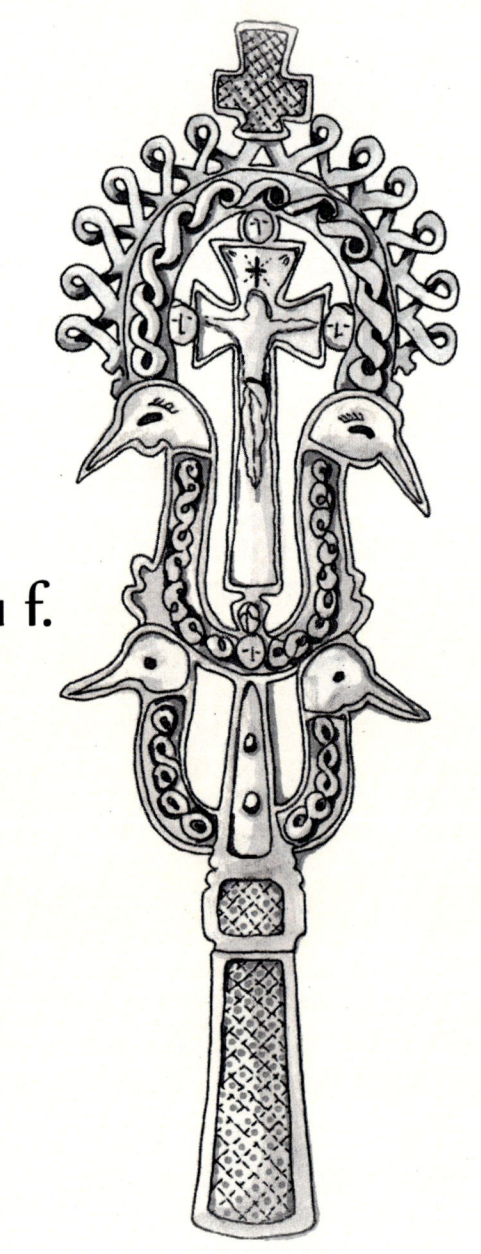

About the Story

The rock-hewn churches of Lalibela, Ethiopia are a UNESCO World Heritage Site. Their history is so ancient that no one knows exactly how the churches were carved from the tops of the cliffs with only tools like chisels and axes. It seems that long ago, pilgrimages from Ethiopia to Jerusalem became impossible so King Lalibela set out to build a symbol of the holy land. There are two groups of churches divided by the river Yordannos (Jordan). Tunnels and pathways that connect the churches are also part of the story where people can experience a spiritual journey moving from one part of the complex to the next. Two of the churches have paintings on their walls that show figures such as the king and Saint George, whose church is probably the most beautiful of all the rock-hewn churches.

Photo credit: Matt Andrea

Around 80,000 -100,000 people visit Lalibela every year including many Ethiopian Orthodox pilgrims who flock to the city especially on Ethiopian Christmas and other special days.

Ethiopian girl coming to worship.

About the Author

Jane Kurtz learned to read in Maji, Ethiopia. Many years later, she helped start the not-for-profit Ethiopia Reads, hoping to share book love with young readers in Ethiopia and her own Ethiopian-American grandchildren.

She has published almost forty books for young readers and is on the faculty of the Vermont College of Fine Arts MFA in Children's and Young Adult Literature.

Jane has volunteered with Ethiopia Reads for almost twenty years and now is part of the team creating Ready Set Go Books.

About the Illustrators

Much of the art for this book was donated thanks to art instructors from Clark College ECD (Economic and Community Development). Katie Bradley and Lee Baughman introduced the Ready Set Go books to several of Lee's classes, and as the excitement caught on, other instructors and their classes got involved as well. Students range from beginning painters to experienced artist. Many of the men and women who participated talk about their excitement over being involved in furthering literacy in Ethiopia and bringing joy through their art.

Lee Baughman
Katie Bradley
Debbie Caton
Cheri Gavin
Suzy Foster

Sue Kramer
Tina Mae Fels
Joyce Saulsbury
Joanne Stanbridge
Irina Sztukowski

Some art was donated by Joanne Stanbridge, an illustrator who has supported Ready Set Go Books from its first efforts.

http://www.joannestanbridge.com/

About Open Hearts Big Dreams

Open Hearts Big Dreams began as a volunteer organization, led by Ellenore Angelidis in Seattle, Washington, to provide sustainable funding and strategic support to Ethiopia Reads, collaborating with Jane Kurtz. OHBD has now grown to be its own nonprofit organization supporting literacy, innovation, and leadership for young people in Ethiopia.

Ellenore Angelidis comes from a family of teachers who believe education is a human right, and opportunity should not depend on your birthplace. And as the adoptive mother of a little girl who was born in Ethiopia and learned to read in the U.S., as well as an aspiring author, she finds the chance to positively impact literacy hugely compelling!

About Ready Set Go Books

Reading has the power to change lives, but many children and adults in Ethiopia cannot read. One reason is that Ethiopia doesn't have enough books in local languages to give people a chance to practice reading. Ready Set Go books wants to close that gap and open a world of ideas and possibilities for kids and their communities.

When you buy a Ready Set Go book, you provide critical funding to create and distribute more books.

Learn more at: http://openheartsbigdreams.org/book-project/

Ready Set Go 10 Books

In 2018, Ready Set Go Books decided to experiment by trying a few new books in larger sizes.

Sometimes it was the art that needed a little more room to really shine. Sometimes the story or nonfiction text was a bit more complicated than the short and simple text used in most of our current early reader books.

We called these our "Ready Set Go 10" books as a way to show these ones are bigger and also sometimes have more words on the page. The response has been great so now our Ready Set Go 10 books are a significant number of our titles. We are happy to hear feedback on these new books and on all our books.

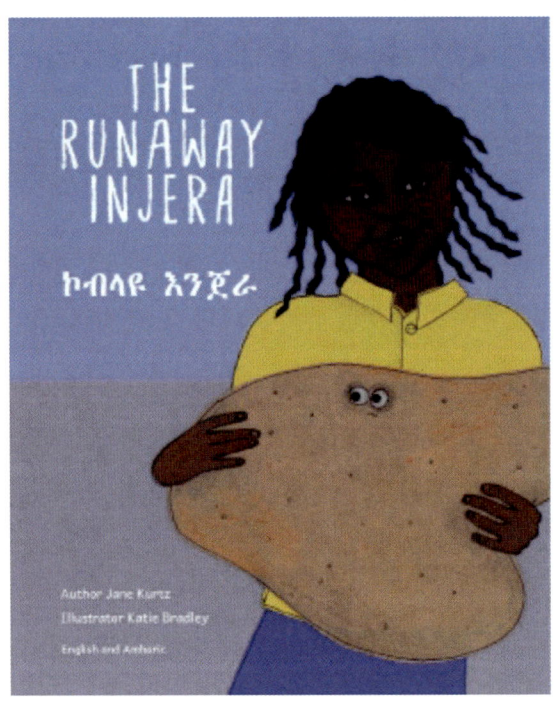

About the Language

The continent of Africa is home to many people who speak Afaan Oromo. Native speakers of Afaan Oromo, in fact, outnumber speakers of every other language except Arabic, Swahili and Hausa. Most Afaan Oromo speakers live in Ethiopia. (Many also live in the United States.) Using the Latin alphabet for writing Afaan Oromo can be traced back to the nineteenth century but was formally adopted in 1991.

About the Translation

Ahmed Dedo Gemeda is an Assistant Professor of English Language and Literature at Haramaya University. He is currently teaching undergraduate and postgraduate students. He is also serving as a translator, editor and reviewer on academic, technical and literary works.

To view all available titles, search "Ready Set Go Ethiopia" or scan QR code

 Chaos

 Talk Talk Turtle

 We Can Stop the Lion

 Not Ready!

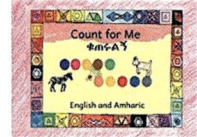 Count For Me

 Too Brave

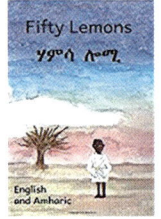 Fifty Lemons

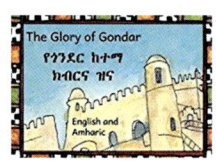 The Glory of Gondar

16479497R00021